THE
LAUNDROMAT
ESSAY

For Lynn –

THE DISAPPOINTMENT OF POETRY.

KYLE BUCKLEY

COACH HOUSE BOOKS, TORONTO

Published with the generous assistance of the Canada Council for the Arts and the Ontario Arts Council. Coach House Books also acknowledges the support of the Government of Ontario through the Ontario Book Publishing Tax Credit and the Government of Canada through the Book Publishing Industry Development Program.

LIBRARY AND ARCHIVES CANADA CATALOGUING IN PUBLICATION

Buckley, Kyle, 1977-
    The laundromat essay / Kyle Buckley.

Poems.
ISBN 978-1-55245-206-6

    I. Title.

PS8603.U325L39 2008   C811´.6   C2008-906013-X

for R

'The disappointment of poetry.'
Steve McCaffery

I know the owner of the laundromat but can't remember his name, which could be for many reasons. He is closing up the laundromat as I get there.

Possibly the reason for forgetting his name cannot be sought in any special feature of the name itself, but is explained when I remember the subject we were discussing before I was trying to convince him to let me into the laundromat, which I am late getting to. The laundromat owner was asking me about the whereabouts of his son, Hoopy, whom I am familiar with a little but don't feel comfortable discussing with the laundromat owner since it isn't my business. If I try to think of the name of the laundromat owner, this new train of thought, I'm sure, would disturb its predecessor, since I am now interested in trying to get the laundromat owner to let me past him into the laundromat, which is now closed. I can no longer regard the fact that I forget the name of the laundromat owner as mere chance.

The Animal Poem

There are many animals in the play,
so most of the actors will be required
to play animals as well as people.

When any of the animals die onstage, it should
be accompanied by the sound of a tape rewinding.

Landscapes

Growing up, we were all part of the structure. We thought the structure was a painting. There was Dad counting our blessings by the number of things people said, and Mom writing them all down. It was the only thing we had for a photo album.

The conversation with the laundromat owner starts the same way that my last **conversation** with you did. A conversation starts with what Ashbery calls 'brittle, useless **architecture**' that affords a high but teetering, scaffolding-like vantage point of the action. What happens during the course of the conversation with you draws an irreproachable map of the city. It's the conversation that I'm always trying to get back to, that I'm always trying to find you in. What seems to be keeping me off track is that architecturally, at this moment, the poem dramatizes a confrontation with the laundromat owner across the street from my apartment.

We were invisible cats. A tiger's latent speed is its disappearability. At lunch we got five extra minutes of TV when the soup was too hot. Then at dinner we found tufts of orange fur in the cuts of meat on our plates. The light in the kitchen stayed on all winter. Someone's mother always coming downstairs and saying oh, she wished she'd had someone to stay up and talk to like you kids. Taking leftovers from the fridge. That year old Tigerman had a vague cancer. A kind that causes crying. Reduces to the appetite of a house cat. He died after that but we still see him. He said he had California inside him the size of his heart.

I can't tell the laundromat owner anything about his son, which, I think, is because a **poem** is a sequence in which images are undivided, even by the architecture itself. You have to be inside all of that undivision. In theory, this all occurred to me because, after all, the poem is in the moment that names and bodies fail. It occurs to me that I think that's exactly why I can't say where his son is; I have a precursory course of thought, which could get disrupted. And then what, I'm left to wonder. After all, I'm just back in the city. I found my apartment in the same state of half-repair as I left it. The shelves were down in the kitchen, leaves had blown in. (I've taken beams down from the ceiling to build a stair-case right down to the street, or a table, I'm not sure which.) But when I'm back in my apartment, I just end up taking on all of the anxiety of pacing around what seems like an obstacle course. I wanted to unwind from my trip, but I seemed to be in a bad place for all of this. I lay down on a couch that I've half-built into a specifically beautiful but impractical ramp. It's a working ramp, but it allowed me to fall into nothing but an unrestful sleep. I doubt I had any dreams, or remembered even a strand of anything to write down. Before I slept, I had practically cajoled myself out of the clothes from my trip, convincing myself with that act to throw almost all of the clothes, everything else I packed for the trip, almost all the clothes I own, really, into the washing machines at the laundromat right across the street from my apartment. I have to consider that had been contributing to the fact that I'd woken up in a state of unease. All of this being a precursor for the disruption I was about to feel at the laundromat.

1988: J and I had memorized scripts for talking on the phone. I spoke our secret code for asking if J would come over. After eating too much of what we decided on later as our favourite animals, we both felt bad. This found us in the shelter at the park deciding we'd find new things to eat that nobody had thought of. That first unrest of hunger.

1989: My dad saw me with B down by the ravine. In the alluring difficulty of constant heat and the pervasive sounds of insects, we were amending familiar things, making the grass mean mud, and the rocks mean pools of water. We included any grasshoppers that we could catch. But had to scramble to get our clothes back on. Like an arithmetic adding us up.

1990: She suffered a kind of collapse. Feeling deserted, paralyzed with the fear of not being able to move. We all had to help her take those first steps again, slowly and cautiously relearning to walk. And love builds a perpetually collapsing house with the resilience of a soap bubble.

1991: We met in the forest on the way down to the quarry, S and I. The rocks shone silver, catching from overhead the stars breaking open. Older lessons than geography emanating. A storm against the night sky and light rain. We go back to my house and sneak in by the light of the television from the living room. The flashes of lightning and the TV both soft and pulsive.

As I pace my apartment, I have this abandoned poem stuck in my head, I can't remember from **when**. *Stuck as we were in those sad intervals of life.* 'Stuck as we were,' I catch myself saying out loud, at this point roaming the various obstacles of my apartment (I've woken up in a state of disruption), 'in those sad intervals of life.' And with little else to do except climb out onto the roof and listen to our favourite songs; it's amazing what we could do with all our old ideas we had been using for television.

Childhood poems seem bathed in television light. Ultimately I abandon them. Like we didn't even have television yet. It was the nostalgia for invention. We had TV sets with blank screens because no one had thought to invent the signals.

A manuscript of poems that both imitates the structure of a cohesive narrative and denies it by enjambing fragmented segments of narrative as well as portraying recurring events with various outcomes on both memory and immediate action.

The biology of prisms, I figured. And I laid these things out in stars on the floor. It spelled a constellation, *we owe our bodies to science.* You came home and smiled at me carefully. As you put it, hearts might be breaking too fast around here. You slipped me something to make me fall asleep. Then, sitting down at the table beside me, you started making corrections to a copy of a poem★ that earlier I had almost finished writing down. As you so delicately put it. We had to quite carefully imagine ourselves.

★The changes you made to the poem involve a boy throwing starfish out again. Tired of them filling up the kitchen sink. As it turns out, the word *suddenness* had started to work like inertia. On our way home we used to pull nets of those starfish behind us on our bikes. It got slower and slower to pedal.

I pace my apartment with the curious anxiety of the moment when you hear a song played twice in the same set by mistake. I feel like I want to get dressed and go out. From the scaffolding-like vantage point of my apartment, the view of the laundromat across the street remains the only certain coordinate of my gesture towards **getting something finished**. I want to get my clothes back from the laundromat. I don't want to end up disrupted from my original course of action. I might be at loose ends, but I feel like I have something to do that can't be separated from my whole compulsion to keep moving.

Something about **you** that is almost stabilizing to me is that we are in a state of constantly returning to a conversation that is never finished. I imagine a maze. I imagine that the routes to get back to you are still being drawn, so I don't know how long I'll be gone. It's the same for any route you might take. So I don't know how long to wait. I imagine young architects in love in the city, in fountains washing the sleep of their exhaustive educations from their tired faces. If, I imagine, you are at the square by the memorial clock at eleven, I'm at the revival hall. At midnight I'm by the bridge out of town, you are in a downtown train station. I imagine, without any concern to how near you are, not reaching you, because even when you would speak my name from the next room I had to somehow get across a dangerous and broken hallway, on the precariously confused description of a broken ladder. It seems that my apartment is really a bad place for all of this. Night starts to fall in through the window and I have to go out.

Plates falling like stars. I write, 'We drive out to where we can watch the meteor shower. It's never long before I tell you I have to go. Get some work done. I make my way back home and change all of the clocks to show a time when we could both listen at more possible speeds. I start the car again and go out to find you. The headlights show the bits of meteor that have settled over everything.'

When I present myself in front of the laundromat, I'm met by the laundromat owner. I find myself trying to implore him to let me into the laundromat to get my clothes. Instead, his figure blocks the door entirely. It is not one of those times that I have shown up late at the entrance to the laundromat and taken out my own front-door key, tried irrelevantly to use my key on the door to the laundromat, and perhaps pushed my key back into my pocket so I could try to proceed as if I hadn't made the mistake in the first place. This time, the owner himself refuses me entrance back into the laundromat unless I answer his questions about whether or not I might know where his son, Hoopy, might be. They'd had a **falling** out over the business.

There is despite everything an effort to sustain a narrative voice, even past the point of the boundaries of body and name.

He says his son won't **speak** to him. Won't see him, and now is nowhere to be found. 'We had a terrible fight,' the laundromat owner tells me. He explains how his son had come barging in one day with his far-fetched plans to expand the business. 'I said he had no head for that sort of thing, but he persisted and persisted. "This old building might fall down one day," he said to me. "When the bricks fall down from the outside walls, when the bathtub from the apartment upstairs overflows and water leaks through everywhere, your repair bills are going to cost more than the laundromat could make even if everyone was doing as much laundry as if they were all throwing in the clothes they were wearing in their dreams the night before when they were on their way to work every morning."' It occurs to me just how incredulous the laundromat owner is when he speaks about his son.

However, I have to regard the laundromat owner carefully as I try to best position myself to my own advantage. I think maybe that by listening intently to him I can move in a slow orbit towards that advantage. As I listen to him talk about his son, I consider trying to start a nearly mechanical rotation, silently entreating the laundromat owner to move in unison with me until we would have switched places and he would no longer be standing between the door to laundromat, through which I could go and retrieve all of my clothes from the wash, and myself. In that way we would have become simply another one of the moving parts, breathing and talking parts, of the city. We would turn on an axis of neutrality. And all of the axes in the city turn on neutral things. *Axis* is a word that carries me along on my course of action, which I'm trying not to let get derailed, while it similarly carries the laundromat owner forward as he talks about his son.

Love wouldn't lessen. This love constitutes a kind of sequel to literary theory. The detotal of my thoughts of my grandmother, who passed away, but hadn't when I wrote this poem, is called 'Wolfmother.' I added a foot-note from another poem. A fragment of a fragment.

Wolfmother

I am very sullen about it. And I will not
eat any of the breakfast my grandmother has
made for me. 'Well I don't care, you're not going
out to hunt those animals again today. T-u-f-f.'

That's not how you★ spell *tough* I mutter, and go
upstairs to stalk the pictures in magazines.
I find an article about what airplanes think of
fighter pilots.

★Later, about the time when I gave you a copy of a book I was reading,
we watched fledgling airplanes stretch their unsteady wings and flex their
plastic windows. They took their first little jumps into the air. Learned to
drift like snowflakes.

The reason why I keep on about the axis, the place it holds us in, is all in my head. It is what prompts me to turn, given the momentum of my own narrative, and face you. Or, rather, it insists on itself as the reminder of my own neutral poem:

'My old **grandfather** is dying. I don't know yet about a new one. Mr. Wolfe is the only one who has been around. He's shown an interest in some of the paperwork. There is a lot of organizing and reorganizing to be done. One time, my grandfather devised a type of camera that lets you invent your childhood. I can make you show up as faintly as tracing a promise. Going through some old boxes, we find a prototype. Turning it on, I take a picture of you putting all your beliefs in storm clouds. Behind you, in the sky like lightning, a picture of everything you want shows through.

'When the news comes, we're caught distracted. Then who should show up with an authoritative clearing of his throat as he cleans his glasses, puts them back on and looks at us both like he was the attorney. This Mr. Wolfe will take some getting used to.'

Wolves put up poems covering the whole wall. The removal of syntax causes the sound of breaking glass in four walls around us. For your birthday you wanted an orange box. I wanted to put up something to remind you of a time when you invented an old television you used to take to bed. Eventually it began to stutter some pictures and sounds. So I put a calendar together.

The presence of the wolves prompts a rupture in any chronology, a small amount of blood in the machine. A succession of words rests as stilled grammar over a field. When you take memories and pull out the syntax, you'll hear the sound of breaking glass.

Instead of completing the slow turn on an axis that would grant me access to the laundromat, the owner stops me where I stand. He holds out his arms. In this way he captures me in my stopped orbit and I am caught with no choice but to listen, with him still keeping me from getting inside the laundromat. 'He said to me,' the laundromat owner continues, still talking about his son, 'we have to get in the movies. He told me we can put our laundromats in movie theatres. People want to be at the **movies**, and they would do their laundry there if only we give them the opportunity.'

Every structure is like the simile of remembering. You are wearing a black turtleneck while everyone else wears suits tailored to wolfish styles. You walk out of the house. Outside it is night.

You turn to a projection on the back wall of the interior. It is a movie of everything I know about you.

Those old movie theatres have all been given such beautiful restorations. They might still look like **old buildings** from the outside, but inside they are all new. Maybe allowing some consideration to the design, there could be a suitable rental space in which the laundromat could set up. The people could wash their clothes while they watch a screening. Film is something **I know a little bit about.** And it can be such a seductive medium. I can almost see some validity to the plan.

The Wolf-Rayet Star*

Poetry is a negation or succession of negations over a field. It's machinery in which stars grind to a halt. The wolf's presence is autological. The sky: an external loudness. Our work gets done finally with the momentary occurrence of a room on the inner side of us. We use a stilled grammar that can be liquefied to almost a phosphorous paint.

You want to paint the floor again, illustrating a family of stars that glow blue on the floor's atmosphere. They're believed to be unstable and short-lived. Because, you explain, we don't understand the capacity of carbon memory.

In our backyard we discovered an anaesthesia mine. Our old TV didn't have a static dream left in it so we buried it there.

*The Wolf-Rayet star was discovered last year from the back of a car with a flashlight. Rayet was a psychologist who claimed there was an anatomical origin for stars.

'He was calling me an old man,' the laundromat owner carries on. 'I said to him that he **doesn't** know what he's talking about. He has never even learned the business. All he ever wants is to be in the movies. You would think that's the answer to everything. It's always, "We should be in the movies." All of the time.' But I'm pretty sure Hoopy was trying to make the point that he had, in fact, very much learned the business, when he stormed out of the laundromat that last time, grabbing some folded sheets from a well-stacked pile of clean laundry and almost parachuting from the **family's** refurbished and partially automated business enterprise.

The mnemotechnology prompts you to increase the vocabulary of your loneliness. The soft stereo plays the folded home-repair surfaces of forgetting. In order to repair what you already know, you pause and record.

We fail to reach an understanding, the laundromat owner and I. Neither of us is able to get past the other. We are always forgetting, as if forgetting were like the mechanized version of everything we failed at in conversation. Although sometimes I'm not comfortable with any analogy I've ever made, my thoughts are about the recent trip out of the city. The country air might have done me some good, but it made me want to get right back to where I was to begin with. As far as today goes, here is some of what has been presented (probably falsely) as part of my recent work on analogies:

'We take your cousin R for a drive, when your cousin says, "Stop the car, I can't feel my arms and legs." We have to stop and get out. The driver, who is also your business manager, is able to set up a TV tray by the side of the road with a fax machine on it, so we can send off some of the new song lyrics we've been thinking up. Because nothing, as we said to ourselves, is like these country drives for getting at least our new ideas for songs circulating.

'All the while, still coming from the car **stereo**, the band Stereolab has been playing, like a kind of abhorrent but stingingly spiritual beauty. Like the kind of beauty that carries violence. The violence that dictates the length of a poem.'

A difference between us bridged my fondness for a
street that ran through the kitchen. It was evenly lined
with the trees that line those kinds of streets. That
autumn we had to gather the leaves from the floor.
They fell when you quietly pulled down the shelves
from inside the cabinets.

The strand of a voice over a PA system starts to sing in cosmic
country noir.

But aside from any of this, I want to **argue** with *you* instead of the laundromat owner. If you were here, I could tell you, 'I remember when *beauty* was a neutral word. Like when you were a beauty living at the edge of town. I thought of a way to convince you to move back to the city that involved an elaborately configured moving skyworks. Which you could be attached to by a hook as part of a newly configured spine (which is ironic because spine was the only part of your body that I wanted to be for you). This is my recent work. And once you had travelled on the skyworks all the way back into the city, we could get you set up with an apartment and I could give you a job in a newly conceived-of postering campaign (which might involve elongated arms or wrists).' But it's all just something to say.

Once I told you to think of me as if I'd just driven out to where you'd been working and found your particular work station beside a stream, amidst an interworking of outdoor conveyor-belt assembly lines, but you weren't very inter-ested in my new sky or coming back to the city at all. As I turned to head back to my car, I heard you **say** softly but certainly, 'You can go, but just don't leave me.' I turned back around and faced you standing there with outstretched arms. Everyone then turned from their various stations along the assembly lines, no longer concerned with their work, held their arms out the same way and said in unison, 'You can go, but just don't leave me.'

Recent graphic formations underlying the surface of our living room furniture illustrate the historic moment when both wolves and airplanes demonstrate their ability to watch TV.

We arrive at home while we're right in the middle of figuring all of this out. Having invented a clock that matches time to feelings, we have tried what it's like to show up at different times. Maybe the TV should get out more. Anyway, the feeling of the electronic glow fills us to the walls of the room.

A manuscript of poems that function like personal essays. Each essay has at least two beginnings.

An essay composed of scenes of delay, and the narrative of fracturing memory.

And I don't have **time** to argue with the laundromat owner because I've only just returned from a trip, having realized that it broke my heart to leave the city. Or really that it broke whatever wasn't broken in the city already. I would explain to him about getting back to the city, about having to find you, except that I think sometimes we have to **edit** our reasons for things. This becomes another scene depicting a dramatic return: I get back to this very **broken** city and I'll go out to find you. I will find you at a public monument, I will find you on a vast flight of cracked concrete stairs, tumbling apart.

I have a fever on the floor of my room, so I write you a letter there on the improvised idea of a typewriter. On the other hand, ideas seemed to turn rapidly back into the machines they came from. Someone else must have gotten the letter, so I get up to find you.

Just like in the grammar of film, there are interspersed scenes of us trying to get home. We're followed by little birds made of vaudevillian origami that are like folded paper learning to chirp. We disguise ourselves as wheat inspectors and keep to the side streets, resorting to escalators down the outsides of office buildings. Everyone keeps words under their hats.

I'll be there to find you but I'll **look ridiculous** because the laundromat owner hasn't let me get my clothes, so I'm wearing whatever outfit I could put together. What I have on would be the hypothetical equivalent of something like a faded, matted sweater, almost colourless, and pants with some kind of stripe down the side, like part of a band costume. And ill-fitting. It's accurate to describe whatever I'm wearing as vague. This description is really so that I can make the analogy that it's like I'm wearing a Joseph Beuys felt suit. (It's a multiple. Who knows which one of the copies of the suit I'd be wearing, but I would have it hanging on the wall from an ordinary coat hanger.)

I thought you and I should understand the life of furniture better than we did, so I brought some wooden beams down from the ceiling, which I could use to build a table. I started to tell you that we preferred rain in the house to mineral water.

The suit was hanging a little high up on my wall, but I needed something to wear, so I got a small ladder out to get it down. The ladder was around because of the **work** I was doing around my apartment, while my clothes were all at the laundromat because I'd just gotten home from a trip and had nothing left to wear and the laundromat owner wouldn't let me back into his laundromat to get them because he said it was too late, they were closed. But he had his own reasons for not letting me back in.

I think of a time when my grandfather reached out with a glass jar, like it held the word *moth* inside. It went across the presence of grammar then.

Imagine a blind clock. With no hands.
You* have to touch it to know that it's there.

*During a lecture on amnesia:
The mechanism for erasure is an individual part of every pronoun. But you and I have a map and a clock.

I put it on. The jacket comes down a little long, or maybe the sleeves come up a little short. It's all one colour of felt, and wearing it is like what Celan says is the **hopelessness of black silk**. Except it's different because it's made of grey felt, not black silk. It might feel at first like it's as formless as one draped piece of fabric made from silk so silklike that you lose your hopeless but beautiful breath. But it's not that formless, since it's cut like a normal suit. It makes a felted image that can be explained but not described. (In the suit pockets you can find, typed on strands of crumpled white paper, the notes from a lecture on **amnesia**.)

Monday

My father waits for me outside my apartment and
instead of talking to him I lock the door behind me.
You're there.

You were waiting inside for me with your book
of silver leaves of carbon memory. You tell me that
my father and I used to play that music for the kitchen
dancers, always on Sundays. The last time we danced
I had to move the table and chairs out of the way
just to make room and the dancers kept
standing on each other's feet.

I feel the compulsion to start **talking**, almost to you, but almost to make it clear that you are not standing in front of me. I want to finish the lecture written in the pockets of the felt suit. I want to explain to you that while the story describes poetry, it also explains why I fail to write it so thoroughly. I'm not sure how to say it, but the failure is so comprehensive.

'A man who employs me,' I catch myself saying out loud, 'named Mr. Delouit, would ask me to look up books on his more esoteric productions. He calls me and asks, "What was I doing in Europe as much ten, fifteen years before I asked you last? It might have been in Paris, 1985. I recall something in a hotel room. Check the footnotes for strange occurrences in the shopping journals of the time. Search the catalogues for something of interest that could have been in the newspaper headlines. In those pages of carbon memory."'

Chameleon-like. The technology of consideration might creep.

Consider incompleteness as a founding concept of the technology of theory.

'What are the names of animals?' 'Chameleons.' Your forehead flickered again like a moth going back to its parents. Every time I read the information, I try not to love it less. It gets louder and out of focus, like a headache that is inside the information itself. My brother remembers a time when the information was replaced by the noise of machinery grinding to a halt, as a series of negations.

Mr. Delouit would stay on the phone, half singing, while I looked up records of his work, his productions across Europe, in the domestic spaces of Paris, or anywhere else. And he'd ask me, 'What are the names of animals?' '**Chameleons**,' I told him. Their eyes are so distinctive among the reptiles. The upper and lower eyelids are joined, the eyes can rotate and focus separately to observe two different objects simultaneously. It in effect gives them a full 360-degree arc of vision around their body. Both eyes can be focused in the same direction, giving sharp stereoscopic vision and depth perception. They have very good eyesight for reptiles. The information becomes beautiful.

This story doesn't describe what I'm wearing, however, since I certainly don't remember what I'm wearing (even though I think it was originally called 'The Description of Clothes'). But it does explain where I'm going. I find myself nearly pushed out of my apartment by the force of following my own flight of stairs down to the street outside. I go into the city, into the anxious heart of it all. I go into the city to move around in it.

The verb tense for paraphasia comes into creation when an action coincides with not remembering. For instance, in a filmed sequence that incites this 'phasic' confusion, you are putting funeral clothes on over the clothes that you wear already.

We get a lesson in ontology when my brother and I spend the night catching fish. There are small diamonds in the fish. We choke when pieces of diamond get stuck in our throats and cut deeply when either of us tries to swallow. Lightning across the whole sky and rain. The sound of thunder fills up around us. A fluorescent light emanates from the water. It newly bathes the scene. We have to call for help.

But now it's like I'm wearing a **suit** that can make it look like whenever I change the direction I'm walking in, I will still find myself somewhere I know in the city. It's like I'm wearing a suit that draws an irreproachable map of the city around me. And then in the void left by any explanation, I start to explain, yet more **ambiguity** rushes in. You know, like thunder.

I find out that if I keep a calendar then the details can always change and I can remember everything. And this way it can all go together. For instance:'1987: My old grandfather had a vague cancer that year. A kind that causes crying. Reduces to the appetite of a house cat. He died after that but we still see him. He said he had California inside him the size of his heart.'

The unpoetics of space are increasing, so the partly sympathetic should consider an architectural validity of concept. Concept is a pliable concept.

For instance, I find myself in front of a bank machine. It happens to be the same machine I make frequent withdrawals from, close to where my apartment is, and to the laundromat. I mean to search my pockets for my bank card. Fumbling through the few **vague** personal effects I find that I'm carrying, I settle accidentally and distractedly on my house key. I've got to find my bank card instead. Anyway, I have plans for an elaborate postering campaign that I'm hoping will take me across the whole city **and back**. All I need is some start-up money for supplies and to get things moving.

Simultaneously causing us to remember separate times of this slow grind of feeling. Meanwhile, we are in the slow grind towards feelings.

I'm forced to pause, though, even when the machine already has my card. I can't remember my card number, the number I'm prompted to enter. I think I'm distracted by my plans for posters that will be lettered to read 'Brittle, hopeless architecture' or 'Our scaffolding-like vantage point.' These posters will really mark out that irreproachable map. (Although with my slogans going through my head, and not being able to remember my bank number, I'm forced to **pause** at the bank machine, and it occurs to me that I'm forced to pause again.)

Monday feels like you and I keep waking up from correction after correction. One after another they get stored in a bank.

It was a mistake to **repeat** the word *pause*, I should have said something like 'forced to pause, even to stall' while I worked on remembering. But I was only trying to keep my thoughts on other things while I tried to remember my card number, so that, inadvertently, I might remember while I am otherwise distracted. I might have been thinking about how to get my posters everywhere I want them in the city. The whole city could read like it was built from scaffolding, leaning over to touch you with a memory of hopeless beauty.

In the poem, they build bridges out of each grammar.

MY GRANDFATHER: Each grammar constitutes a mechanism, you know. You and I are here for talking and meanwhile a room speaks for itself. After this room, two nights will follow.

MR. WOLFE: (Clears his throat.)

MY GRANDFATHER:

MR. WOLFE: (The grammatical mechanism for non-accomplishment.)

But when nothing works, when what I'm trying to remember won't come to me, it starts to rain. Trying just to get my hands to remember something, I put in part of a phone number I used to call, or any numbers that I seem to remember for some reason. Something seems to work. It rains on my hands as I hold them out at the keypad. As I put the small sum of money away (you always have to have some money in the city, but I've been sufficiently distracted from my elaborate postering plans), I return my card to my pocket. I hold my hands out again. It rains on my **outstretched** hands.

There is an ensemble of recurring animal characters. They are representative of a more bureaucratic notion of memory. Whenever grandparents are referred to in any of the poems, they are in a perpetual state of disappearing. The city seems to map itself around places that are familiar to the narrator.

As a stabilizing point to the changing and sometimes competing nature of the narratives in the poems that are rewritten memories, the narrator is constantly returning to the scene of an unfinished and ongoing conversation, the contents of which, and the identity of the other person the narrator is having the conversation with, are never determined within the narrative. The narrator, however, displays a determination to maintain a steady direction towards the completion of narrative.

Moments of narrative are presented that have an ambiguous relationship with each other, one to the next. The narrative almost hangs together but is also in a perpetual state of correction. The architecture of the city, the digressions of the narrative as well as the narrator's ongoing and never-finished conversation culminate in one long poem that carries the echoes of the failed poems within it. *Culminate* might be the wrong word, as the failures of narrative are the very productions of the poem.

Maybe I'm standing here in a felt suit. Maybe it's rained. Maybe the sun's gone down. Maybe I've waited at home and everything has changed course. I went out and traced the map I said was irreproachable, you said was like scaffolding. And it was.

Following the map of the city, I find myself moving in every direction, all of the way to the city's outskirts. I find myself ('For everything that has been said here – ' you started to tell me once, but I think I stopped you from finishing) with a look about me that says, 'This little outcrop might be where you brought me once to show me how the lights from the houses of the neighbouring suburbs illuminate their own particular idea of the city.' Then I hear a voice over a PA system (I don't know if there was a loudspeaker of any sort, but I know that is what it felt like). It's telling me to turn around and go back into the city.

Maybe it was. I made up this **essay** right here, standing here.

I don't recall if Ashbery has a poem about the analogy between beauty and violence. Nor do I recall listening to something like darker country music, or if the scene was lit with as much seduction as surprise. Since it is night and the entire scene is side-lit with a gentle wash of beautiful white electric light, there is no reason to consider whether or not changes in the lighting direction, as well as our position relative to the light, have a tremendous impact on our appearance as architectural subjects.

This becomes another scene of dramatic return: I get back to this very broken city and go out to find you. It is at this public monument that I find you on this vast flight of cracked concrete stairs, tumbling apart. This is a difficult scene to visualize because our heights are very possibly distorted, depending on if I'm taller than I would normally be because I'm standing on a higher stair than you or vice versa and you're even taller because you're on a higher stair. Or can it, given the state of disrepair of the stairs, be safely determined that the stairs even climb on one steady slope in one steady direction? So even though I think the poem was originally called 'On Whether Ashbery Has a Poem About the Analogy between Beauty and **Violence**,' I think this poem could be attributed to my new theory about how two bodies can express 'architectural advantage.'

Swimming

Wanting to know where the ideas come from, we ended up at a clearing at the edge of the water under a rising moon. We had soap underneath our fingernails; we had carved the stars out of it. Sharks nearby just beneath the surface. They swim an intricate flight pattern. An exciting danger to them. Later on, your sister sort of phased out and then back into things for a time. Nice to have her with us, though, while she was.

At night we drove to the airport. Which was spectral. An astral landing strip spreads out before you from the highway. The airplanes teach their young to swoop and fly over the deserted stretch. They come down low enough to fly right beside you. The title was either Migrations or The Imaginations of Sharks.

By this point, I very nearly love you. Which means that I love you with, I don't know, all of the intensity of a thousand brilliant suburban porch lights. These are the kind of lights that surround each of us at some point in our lives, and are so near to almost everything. And thoughts like this seem to trail off, just as at one point the moon was so big that for a short time it actually held us in place. And goddamn it if meaning wasn't shining its face in our goddamn eyes. Dad kept on with his emancipation of the lawn-mower engine anywhere a lawnmower might go. Mom had her way too.

I know that any analogy has to be at least one-half familiar. Recently I've been working on what kind of lighting effect can be most familiar concerning a certain kind of nostalgic memory loss. Questions unfold like anesthetic leaves. (You ask me late at night about how I could catch horses. I counted six that I chased through your backyard and they jumped fences. Four, you tell me, there were four horses that day you brought them to school. We rode them through the halls, sure to find evidence of low tide.) My memory is finally iconoclastic enough. But these are some of the best memories I can think of because, after all, it's a play. And because I'm always paying for it all with my heart. It's been said, 'Where can I go and pay for what I need based on my false memories alone and nothing else,' and I couldn't agree more.

I don't remember everything correctly, but I don't want to lie to you. Because I very nearly love you. Deeply, even jealously, I want to tell you something. Because I have a compulsion to tell you.

Nightjar

Your glass face. Such that those small muscles around your mouth and eyes shine quite specifically. It's not so much that you said I should leave as it was this statue of a pool of shining water. I see it on my way out to the airport, to go somewhere. From my window on the plane, the same statue looks like a metal bird. From my unsteady vantage point as an ornithologist, it reads: *we cannot eat with metal birds on our plates.* The feeling of my forehead touching a pane of glass lasts for only so long. Fields below number in the twenties.

I have this and much more to tell you. By the time I turn around, I get back and find you in the yard. I bring out a flashlight to help you plant tiny machines in the garden. This way we can pull the little things out of their shells and put them into shells of our own. You've decided on this. And everything else has to wait.

Wolf Factory

It seems everything happened at night down at the wolf factory. Where the grind of the machines manufactured an impassive silence. As they moved about their assembly lines, I carved a sentence out of metal with your name and the words *leaving at the time of night.* This drew some strange looks from the wolves, but they kept their distance and everyone got along fine.

Once I just kept working there at the factory after you were gone. It was all like a scene right out of a film about the evening news. When you came back, you found everyone sitting in the factory living room watching TV. An uneasy reunion, but I gave you the sentence that I'd made. You put it into the empty suitcase you were carrying. You'd gotten only as far as the airport.

As we've found ourselves saying before, we didn't really ever talk about much. The reason for this is quite possibly that we never finish our conversation. But I feel I can draw you a map of what it is like to have something to tell you. I can tell you about trying to get back to you, trying to get to the airport, trying to get home, waiting for you. I can tell you in different ways, following these different maps. I think of all these as great possibilities and yet still as subtle, beautiful failures. I wrote you out a map titled '**Variations on getting out to or getting back from the airport.**' I have this much to tell you.

On the subject of getting out to or getting back from the airport, I first considered something more geometric. The biology of prisms, I figured. And I laid these things out in stars on the floor. It spelled a constellation, *we owe our bodies to science*. You came home and smiled at me carefully. As you put it, hearts might be breaking too fast around here. You slipped me something to make me fall asleep. Then, sitting down at the table beside me, you started making corrections to a copy of a poem★ that earlier I had almost finished writing down. As you so delicately put it. We have to quite carefully imagine ourselves.

★In the copy of the poem, I am waiting for you to come home. It begins, as Ashbery says, with 'brittle, useless architecture' and I couldn't agree more. My apartment affords a high but teetering, scaffolding-like vantage point of the action. It dramatizes a confrontation with the laundromat owner across the street from my apartment. I know the owner of the laundromat but can't remember his name. While I'm waiting for you, I go out to a restaurant and eat. Afterwards, I get back and fall fast asleep. I dream that everything happens the exact same way. The poem starts with 'I don't recall if Ashbery has a poem about the analogy between beauty and violence … ' You come home.

As part of your abstract research, consider a blindfolded airplane pilot. Speaking into an empty cabin. This book is like a blindfolded staircase.

Meanwhile, you and I are still, as it is, undivided within the image itself of 'architectural advantage' (and remember that we started from a point of view of a certain amount of architectural frailty, instability), which puts into play the kind of confusion that represents the only things that have the capacity for much in the way of actual beauty in the **manuscript**. Those are lighting effects, a kind of nostalgic memory loss, the tone of voice of the narrative, which is maybe in your own head, and I think there's music too. So there are those things. And on those stairs it occurs to me, in this advantaged confusion of two bodies, that the only people who truly care what other people think about them are the very beautiful themselves.

Then you say that I've already told you this before. And I ask, 'All of this? About the stairs … '

By this point you had made yourself into several differ-
ent people. As such, I was probably one of those separate
people. We were talking about you. One thing about
you is you have always projected a sense of certainty.

'You told me a story from André Breton's *Nadja*,' you say. 'It was about a man named Delouit. And M. Delouit, while staying at a hotel, informs the desk that, because he has no memory at all, each time he comes in he'll tell his name, M. Delouit, to whoever is at the desk. And every time he'll need to be told his room number all over again. This happens once, but then moments later, the same man, though much more dishevelled, appearing maybe even to be injured, comes in through the front doors of the hotel and tells his name to the desk: M. Delouit. "What do you mean? M. Delouit has just gone upstairs." He answers, "I'm sorry, it's me. I've just fallen out of my window. What is the number of my room please?"'

Delouit. Delouit. Suddenly, it occurs to me that I will never remember the laundromat owner's name. I had just come back from a camping trip with his son, Hoopy. He and my brother and I had spent the night catching fish, but my brother choked on a small piece of diamond in the fish that got stuck in his throat and cut him deeply when he tried to swallow. My brother had to be taken away. I think Hoopy had just taken an apartment in the west end.

But we know that replacement is deeply seeded in the process of forgetting. For instance, right then I didn't remember you telling me that my piano teacher was always waiting for me outside my apartment because he and I used to play music for the kitchen dancers always on Sundays. The last time we danced I had to move the table and chairs out of the way just to make room and the dancers kept stepping on each other's feet. And it's Sunday.

I have this and much more to tell you. But by the time I ever get back to you, you're out in the yard. I bring a flashlight to help you plant tiny machines in the garden. This way we can pull the little things out of their shells and put them into shells of our own. You've decided on this. And everything else has to wait.

In theory, by this point, I had forgotten about you so completely, it starts to rain again. By 'theory,' I mean 'no theory has yet succeeded in giving a full account of the phenomena of **remembering** and forgetting.'

But we know that interference is deeply seeded in our process of forgetting, which in turn is caused by interference to the information we are being given to act on and the course of actions themselves. Sometimes new associations to a familiar compulsion cause some confusion within our otherwise clear desire to carry out a previous response. I am a stalwart of a sky-rigged mechanized transportation theory, which lets me put into practice a campaign of postering the city with fragments of what I want to say. This is interference theory.

Or, for instance, this is the theory of me standing here on these stairs, the very stairs I was describing to you just earlier, and it occurs to me that I have been standing here, by this point on my own, for I don't know how long now. I have to go to find you again, and as I turn to do that, I hear a voice over a PA system, and I remember it saying … (I don't know if this was a voice that I actually heard. I don't know if I remember the PA system, but I remember a voice coming over it, starting to talk.) The strand of a voice over a PA system starts to sing in cosmic country noir, 'Did you say love is an artillery shed? I almost forgot.' As it ends, a song starts to play. Slow and dark country music, both dramatic and comforting, music that you have been aware of only peripherally.

As it ends: but that's an old line.

Notes and Acknowledgements

The essay draws from various sources both public and personal. Among them are stolen images from Stereolab's *Margerine Eclipse* as well as from production in my childhood of a play called *Gargoyle* by Robin Fulford, directed by Rainer Noack. The undivided image of poetry is an idea taken from Michel Deguy. Steve McCaffery is quoted from 'Discontinued Meditations.'

Quotations have been misread from John Ashbery's poem 'Clepsydra,' Andre Breton's novel *Nadja*, and an early poem by Paul Celan, 'The next day the deportations about to begin.'

The name Hoopy comes from Jeff Clark's book *The Little Door Slides Back*. Much of this book is otherwise indebted to Freud's *The Psychopathology of Everyday Life*.

I would like to acknowledge support for this book from both the Ontario Arts Council and the Toronto Arts Council.

Too many people are deserving of thanks to be listed here. I would, however, like to express gratitude to the many communities that over the years I have been welcomed into, and have been able to call home. A few of such communities include a faction of the Creative Writing program at York University, Nicole Markotić and the University of Calgary, the lexiconjury, and the literary places I can currently call home, Type Books (with particular thanks to Joanne and Samara) and Coach House Books (with many, many thanks to everyone there, and of course Alana).

Versions of some of the poems in this book originally appeared in *Existere* and the *Queen Street Quarterly* (with special thanks to Stephen Cain). The extraordinarily talented Olia Mishchenko graciously provided the cover illustration.

And I would like to specifically and carefully thank Patricia Buckley, Alana Wilcox and K. B. Thompson.

About the Author

Kyle Buckley lives and writes in Toronto. He works at Type Books and is a past winner of the now-defunct *Queen Street Quarterly* poetry contest. *The Laundromat Essay* is his first book.

Typeset in Bembo

Printed and bound at the Coach House on bpNichol Lane in October 2008

Edited and designed by Alana Wilcox

Cover art by Olia Mishchenko, courtesy of the artist

Author photo by Erin Creasey

Coach House Books

401 Huron Street on bpNichol Lane

Toronto, Ontario M5S 2G5

Canada

416 979 2217

800 367 6360

mail@chbooks.com

www.chbooks.com